It's All About Leadership in Schools...

What works and some of what doesn't!

By

Murry J. Schekman

Copyright 2024 by Murry J. Schekman

All rights reserved. No part of this publication may be reproduced, distributed, or transmitted in any form or by any means, including photocopying, recording, or other electronic or mechanical methods, without the prior written permission of the publisher, except in the case of brief quotations embodied in critical reviews and certain other noncommercial uses permitted by copyright law.

Table of Contents

About the author

Murry Schekman just finished a stint as the Interim Superintendent of Schools of the Pajaro Valley USD, a district of 15,000 students with a large English Learner population, 34 schools, 82% of students living in poverty, 17% having special needs, and 10% identified as migrant students and a staff of 2442. The budget this past year encompassed $361 million. Like other districts, the enrollment has declined 26% since 2015. This final job in his career capped a 40-year career in the world of K-12 and instruction at SJSU. His intent is to capture the essence of effective leadership with real stories – successes and failures on the job and show the link to research-based practices. The target audience is anyone interested in leading in a school environment, and the unintended targets are those who have been in the business a long time and are burned out…. have lost that spark are no longer enthusiastic, for enthusiasm is what can carry us through those impossible moments!

Murry Schekman — a wise and seasoned leader of California schools and districts — speaks with clarity and insight on how to motivate teachers and nurture students. This intimate and inspiring guide to education leadership blends Schekman's rich experience with novel methods for lifting school. This compact book is a must-read for current and future school leaders.

Dr. Bruce Fuller, Professor Emeritus, University of California, Berkeley
Author of '*When Schools Work, Organizing Locally and Standardized Childhood*'

Murry Schekman's '*It's All About Leadership in Schools*' offers a compelling look at effective educational leadership through a blend of personal anecdotes and research. Schekman uses his extensive experience to guide current and aspiring leaders in fostering authentic, supportive, and uplifting school environments. For anyone serving students, this book offers inspiration and practical advice to reinvigorate our passion and impact in education.

Dr. Faris Sabbah, Santa Cruz County Superintendent of Schools

Murry Schekman has provided insight and experience to his students and the faculty at San Jose State University during his time as a senior lecturer in the College of Education. His book provides practical, valuable, and specific ideas for school counselors and leaders at all levels of the K-12 school system. His vast experience combined with the research included herein are valuable assets for anyone interested in expanding their understanding of teaching, counseling and leading at the K-12 level.

Lorri M. Capizzi, Ed.D.

Assistant Professor, Department of Counselor Education

San Jose State University

I dedicate this short book to my family, friends, colleagues and students. All have enriched my life; taught, inspired and nurtured me along the way.

Birds universally represent freedom, transcendence, and spirituality. Birds in flight symbolize freedom as the birds reach heights without having limitations. This symbolism relates to the aspirations of all those involved in educating our young people – the students, teachers, staff, parents and the community!

The running of the bulls is also a symbol for this compact book! The author ran with the bulls in Pamplona, Spain at the age of 20 and has compared it to running schools for most of his career!

Introduction and Intent

In 1973, Murry served as an Instructional Aide in a Special Ed program at O.S. Hubbard Elementary on the East side of San Jose. This article tells the story of leaders, Murry's, and some of the brilliant and less-than-brilliant leaders that he worked with in his career. He served as the principal of six schools -3 middle schools, 2 comprehensive high schools, and a continuation school. He was also a director and assistant superintendent in charge of Secondary Education. He transitioned from K-12 in 2015 to teach full-time in San Jose State University's Administrative Leadership and Counselor Ed Departments. He was invited to come back to his home district and serve as the Interim Superintendent and retired from that position on May 1, 2024. He has a narrative to tell that will include some fun stories, experiences, and research mixed together to help paint a picture of what works in leadership. He began his first presentation with the PVUSD entire Leadership Team at the beginning of the 2023-24 year with a presentation on Leadership, and he ended the year telling the community about his dog and the enthusiasm that he enjoys starting the day with Jesse, his walking companion. So, if you want to learn about the upside and the dark side of leadership in the world of K-12, enjoy this article – *It's All About Leadership in Schools!*

This book intends to guide future educators on the principles of leadership and how to approach it effectively. Its purpose is to share insights on the evolving landscape of education and how to navigate these changes. The book offers practical strategies for designing class schedules, managing discipline, fostering parental involvement, building school culture, preventing burnout, and more. While rooted in research, the core message emphasizes the pivotal role that enthusiasm plays in successful leadership.

Setting the Stage

According to the World Population Review[i]:

- California provided $13,642 per K- 12 student in the school year 2023-24. 19th out of 50 states and the District of Columbia.

- New York leads the nation with $24,881 per student. Other sources provide similar data.

For example, the US News and World Report shows very similar numbers.[ii]

The national scene's divisive nature has dripped into the elections and politics of our "non-partisan" local boards. Alternate realities abound. Some of our K-12 staff are not effective as teachers but play leadership roles in the school's ecosystems. Covid added to the complexities of working toward equity and access for all students. Some of our school leaders are tired and exhausted, and others work to avoid conflicts. These two subgroups of leaders add to our obstacles of moving schools forward to become effective learning places for all students.

Sounds corny! Well, get ready for the real corny stuff! There are so many outstanding and courageous school leaders standing out and getting stuff done on behalf of our kids' learning. Yes, this is an incredibly difficult time to be a leader in a school, and I hope that what I am sharing will help our new (and old!) school leaders look in the mirror and or simply add to their leadership repertoire. I was proud to serve as superintendent of schools in my home district last year. It reinforced the notion that it really is all about leadership! After teaching for nine years at San Jose State in two departments – Counselor Ed and Educational Leadership, I was ready to jump back into the real world of teachers teaching and kids learning AGAIN.

****

I've been fortunate in my career to work with excellent mentors, including veteran administrators, veteran teachers, and gifted college professors. In my younger days, I went by instincts, and sometimes it worked but usually not! Good research and good mentoring led to good outcomes. But it was the enthusiasm that carried the day through the bad times and the good times. I had the privilege of working with so many dedicated and enthused educators. My last year as the Interim Superintendent in the Pajaro Valley USD allowed me to use my repertoire in some difficult situations, but it's the positive culture at the school sites and the enthusiasm that emanated from so many people at the sites and district office that fed my final chapter with joy. So, I want to capture some ideas (and fun, maybe dumb mistakes) in my career and hope to show the links between the real world of classroom learning and proven research practices. Enthusiasm is at the center, and passion is a subset of enthusiasm. Let me add enthusiastically - I would do it all over again!

The Learning Begins –
Way Back When

The year was 1973, and the Vietnam War was winding down, but the aftermath of protest and divisiveness ruled the nation. I was a sophomore at San Jose State and had the good fortune of getting hired at O.S. Hubbard Elementary School on the East side of San Jose- with a very diverse population. I was choosing between journalism, law, and teaching, and this job illuminated the pathway to teaching. I created an alternative movement exploration program for all the kids to go through and then was tasked with keeping the "klutzes" to help them with gross motor skill development. I read a lot and created oodles of alternative movement activities, all fun and engaging. I had no clue what was right or wrong. I had a sense that if the kids improved their gross motor skills and had fun at the same time, it would be a good thing. But 19-year-olds know everything in their heads and very little at all about reality. However, it seemed to have worked. At the end of the year and on my last day, I arrived at the school to see my name on banners proclaiming it was "Murry Schekman Day." The principal gave me a great letter of recommendation, citing my use of Skinnerian behavior modification techniques. I was surprised at their celebration but honored, of course. I left the area to go to the University of

California at Santa Cruz because the view was better than at SJSU. The faculty sent me off with aplomb and a nice faux leather travel bag. I was proud.

It was about 20 years later that I reflected on that experience. At least once a week I took out of every classroom the most hyper students and all at one time. I had no clue that this was taking place. I smiled, realizing that I did help the kids with skill building and esteem, but I knew that the teachers appreciated that hour each week without the kids climbing their walls. Fifty-one years later, I observed more kids "climbing walls" in our school-drug babies, ADHD to the max, kids on the spectrum, and about 5% more special needs kids than when I worked in this district in the 80's.

Tyrone Howard's work "Why Race and Culture Matter in Schools"[iii] wasn't published at that time, but he identifies the essential characteristics of successful schools with large minority populations, much like O.S. Hubbard Elementary.

a. Visionary Leadership

b. Teachers' Effective Practice

c. Intensive Academic Intervention

d. Explicit Acknowledgement of Race

e. Involved Parents and Community

I was fortunate to have visionary leadership at my first K-12 job-both with the teachers who guided me and the principal who guided the kids and adults. His name was Patrick Caporale. The two teachers were Elaine Tremaine and Joan Stoker-Rost. My ideas about teaching, learning, and leadership began there…of course, without realizing it! Before Howard's research, the individuals I worked with practiced 4 of Howard's 5 essential characteristics. Explicit acknowledgment of race was not in the mix in my early career.

Visionary Leadership is an important concept. I've met incredible leaders with excellent vision and the ability to articulate their vision to the school and the community. Unfortunately, I worked with folks who had vision but did not have the ability to express and articulate their vision. One clear and common component of successful leadership included that simple ingredient of enthusiasm.

The Real World of
Leadership

In 1975, I was fortunate to get connected to a brilliant teacher at Aptos High School, Robert Hestand. My colleague from OS Hubbard, Joan Stoker Rost, connected me to Bob. I did not realize it way back when, but those connections paid off with my development and the doors that were opened for me! Mr. Hestand taught Youth and the Law and brought in excellent guest speakers. The speakers represented whatever the issues were at the time in Santa Cruz County. The class was very motivating for the students, and they were engaged in critical thinking activities because of the excellent teaching of Mr. Hestand. The issues were their issues and Bob knew how to teach so they'd learn. His teaching reinforced my beliefs that student learning relevance is critical for students to be engaged. Not all teachers subscribe to this belief. Bob was a master and was highly regarded by his students, his peers, and the community. I was lucky. After one semester of observing it was now my time to take over the class. I was cocky, excited, and thought I was more than ready. I also brought in some excellent speakers, including Leon Panetta, who was in the House of Representatives at the time, and some local County Supervisors, engaging leaders who also wanted to connect with our young people - their future constituents.

One afternoon, a student approached me and let me know he was gay.

I got nervous and unsure of my next step. I asked him why he was sharing this info with me. He let me know that he was happy with the speakers and asked if we could bring in the Gay and Lesbian Union of Cabrillo College. I let him know that I would investigate it with Mr. Hestand. Bob was very happy to see this take place. The district had a Controversial Subjects policy that required permission slips to go home and come back signed before any student could attend the presentation. An alternative lesson was to be prepared if a parent objected. We prepared the permission slips and got ready for the presentation.

There were four panelists, 3 men and 1 woman. One man described himself as a"flamer" based on his dress. The others didn't appear "gay," …but I was young and ignorant. The four of them were gay and proud. They talked about their lives and love, their parents' rejection, and the stigma of being gay. They also talked about their relationships - gay and straight. They showed us that they were just like everyone in the room. The students, Mr. Hestand, and I were very pleased with the presentation and the learning. It was a most successful lesson.

I got a call at home that night that the principal wanted to see me in his office first thing in the morning. Bob let me know that he asked to attend, but the principal declined, and I was meeting the principal by myself!!!! I was nervous. I was 21 years old. I won't name this leader, for he was an ineffective principal. He let me know that he got 300 calls from parents complaining that there were homosexuals on campus and leading a lesson. NONE WERE PARENTS OF STUDENTS IN THE CLASSROOM.

He spent about five minutes yelling and letting me know how bad it was for him…all of those phone calls! His last words for me were, "I'm going to make sure that you never work in the PVUSD!" I served as a teacher, counselor, assistant principal, principal, assistant superintendent, and finally the superintendent of the district. His ability to anticipate my future was wrong. I will talk later about the concept of anticipation, but for now, this is simply about a great teacher willing to take a chance on behalf of his students' learning, a great lesson, and an ineffective principal. It was also about my learning and adding to my teaching and leadership repertoire, whether I was aware of that or not. One of my learnings was that even bad experiences become good experiences over time!

Leadership, in its simplest form, is taking a group of people from Point A to Point B! Unfortunately, at the national level, we have more examples of divisive and ineffective leadership than we have of engaging, inspiring, and leadership that brings folks together with common goals. I will always appreciate the enthusiasm, but not when it is directed toward hate, racism, and exclusion. Enthusiasm is the central theme of this article. I am going to show how our enthusiasm as educators will help to instill hopefulness and opportunities in the lives of our students, their families, AND our employees at all levels. I've seen it in so many places - from the transitional kindergarten classroom to the school cafeteria to the principal's venue and in the community. I've seen parents step up at School Site Council meetings and represent honest and sometimes critical voices. I've seen students come to the microphone at board meetings and talk with great knowledge about their hopes for the Ethnic Studies classes and, at some points, their frustrations with dirty bathrooms. I've seen with pride the hopefulness those students expressed - frustrations but still with the belief that their voice will be heard.

I discovered, fortunately, early in my career, that most of the answers were there right in front of me - usually with the students, staff, parents, and the community for they wanted problems resolved and needed leadership to get in front of the problems and work with PEOPLE for resolution. Cheap cliché – sometimes it's the process that's most important. I worked with a principal who said that if he just had a laptop, a quiet corner, and no disruptions from people, he'd run a great school.

I disagreed.

One of my early role models was Patrick Dooling, an English teacher at a private school and my neighbor in the next classroom. He inspired his students by knowing them as individuals and delivering very engaging lessons. He showed passion in everything he did to help his students learn. He was so passionate that he became a Catholic Priest, and I've had the pleasure of seeing him over the years. I always knew that our jobs had a certain righteousness to them, but meeting Father Patrick years after seeing him teach English was also inspiring!

Now, before you go on, please watch this brief video highlighting Hamish Brewer, a "disruptor" principal. I showed this video to my grad students at SJSU, future counselors, and future administrators. It is a good place for us to go to now in this write-up.[iv]

Mr. Brewer is quite the leader! I appreciate his care and enthusiasm. His high visibility does so much for his school. He is supervising, modeling, and seeing what needs to be done and where! He is enthusiastic in all that he does. The best schools have positive and effective leadership at all levels-classified employees, teachers, counselors, admin, students, and parents.

As you can see, I am trying to engage you with some specific ideas **and** my enthusiasm.

Leadership at a New High School

I was very fortunate to be hired at the new high school in Castroville in 1979, North Monterey County High School - the Condors. I was a Counselor for the Migrant Education program and worked with students and their families who recently arrived in the United States. It was there that I met the Principal, Walt Holmes, who showed many of the characteristics that Mr. Brewer shows us in his video, except without the skateboard.

Walt Holmes car's license plate read "NMCHS#1". He spent the year before the school opened interviewing each of the incoming students. He knew many of the students' names even before they started at this new high school in the middle of the artichoke fields. I started a few months after the school opened and realized that the principal and the entire staff appeared to be on the same page - the advantage for Mr. Holmes and the kids' learning in opening a new high school. The district was blessed with a gifted superintendent, Dr. Dave Tansey, who supported the site in the hiring. NMCHS was a new high school in the northern part of Monterey County. For years, most of the students in Moss Landing and Castroville went to Alisal High School on the east side of Salinas. Although a lawsuit ensued, Mr. Holmes could hire the most qualified staff. He did not have to hire teachers out of Salinas who did not fit the vision that was being created in Castroville. When I arrived, I soon learned that I was surrounded by a very talented and dedicated faculty and staff, and on the same page about the school's vision and culture, or most of the staff anyway! I didn't realize the importance of commonality of purpose way back when, but Mr. Holmes' modeling and quality time with me helped me see the vision and the importance of everyone being on the same page.

Inclusivity, although the word wasn't used back then, was a central theme for the staff at NMCHS. Pride in the new school was built with vibrant activities and an athletics program. The new high school became a source of pride for the community, and I added to my leadership repertoire and learned from all of the staff, but Walt became a mentor until he died at the young age of 51, for he suffered from congenital heart disease. He was the only high school principal who had the privilege of opening TWO new high schools. He left NMCHS and went to Orange County to open Diamond Bar High School - quite an achievement!

Author, teacher, and researcher Anthony Colannino writes in "Leading with Head and Heart" * that ALL MEANS ALL. It's actually the title of Chapter 2. He's referring to the notion that *"Every student, every educator, every leader can learn and grow."* That idea was a central theme of the developing culture of North Monterey County High Schools. But teaching is always a difficult job, and some teachers can't handle the pressure. One day, a group of counselees came to me and complained about a teacher. The teacher got upset with this group of students and let them know that they didn't need to learn in his class because they were going to be operating elevators in the future. It just didn't matter. I talked to the teacher, and he continued to express his frustration. I didn't have enough EXPERIENCE to have a critical conversation. But I did go to the principal and that teacher left the school soon after. I heard he went to law school. Good choice. The principal was quite an enthusiast for his school and he was able to look staff in the eye and have courageous conversations.

Colannino's *Leading with Head and Heart*[v] offers an enjoyable and practical guide to improving the culture of a school. I was blessed to work with such dedicated, talented, and caring people way back when at NMCHS. I was getting my counseling credential and master's degree but changed to Educational Leadership for the master's degree. I earned an admin credential and a counseling credential (Pupil Personnel Services). I already had my teaching credential, and I had passed a few tests, oral and written in Spanish, a few years earlier so I had what was called the Bilingual Certificate of Competence. I worked hard in the beginning - going to school, teaching, and counseling.

It doesn't get easier. But I'm not complaining.

Cultural competence is part of effective leadership. Tyron Howard's description of the effective school in an urban setting includes the explicit acknowledgment of race. The Ethnic Studies requirement in California has brought in difficult and sometimes divisive discussions at local school board meetings. I bore witness to those intense discussions toward the end of my tenure as Superintendent. However, Howard's research relates to the development of an inclusive school culture, welcoming all and having high expectations for all. NMCHS worked toward that culture, and I learned along the way.

One morning I got a call from a neighbor who asked if I oversaw the Migrant Ed program. She let me know that she sees teenagers working in the fields and asked me to do something about it. I wore a tie that day, which I did on occasion. I hung up the call, jumped into my green 1971 Volkswagen Bug, and drove right up to the field parking at the base of the strawberry field. This field of strawberries was on the side of a hill adjacent to one of the district's elementary schools. I got out of my green Volkswagen and saw all the workers running up the hill and away from me. I realized what was going on and yelled out, "No soy la Migra!" None returned. I don't think I reported that story to my colleagues.

This anecdote provides insight and perspective on learning and growing from real experiences, even unexpected or challenging ones, and to recognize when an approach or understanding might be lacking. As I wrote earlier, I learned along the way, and I was very fortunate to be able to learn so much with the help of mentors and experience. Walt Holmes' words and demonstrable enthusiasm were excellent attributes for me to learn from. I learned to appreciate my mentors and recognize the high value they added to my leadership repertoire!

Making A Career Change

I changed my professional goals and my pathway from serving as a school-based counselor to becoming a school administrator! I wanted to be a principal.

After 13 interviews, I landed my first middle school assistant principal job at E.A. Hall Middle School in 1981. The school enjoyed a beautiful facility built in 1932 with the help of WPA funding and artists. Gargoyles adorned the front. Hardwood felt the thump-thump of the middle school shoes and lockers, just like those stereotypes seen on television in the 50s and 60s. Students used the lockers for their books and their personal expressions.

Early on in my career, an 8th-grade student by the name of George burned down one of the boy's bathrooms. He lit a fire in a trashcan filled with paper towels and literally burned the bathroom to the point that the walls were all black, and the fire department cordoned off that wing of the school. My college courses didn't train me how to investigate! Over a short period of time, George had bragged to many of his friends, males and females. Most students want what's right for their family and school and let me know who lit the match! I had enough different witnesses that I moved forward with George. I called him in and let him know we knew he did it and if he had anything to say. He did not. I told him that I was going to call his mother and picked up the phone. As I started to dial George hit himself on the table with his forehead with great force! I froze. He did this two additional times and then pointed to the rapidly forming bump on his forehead and said, "Wait until I tell my mom what you just did to me! "Fortunately, his mother knew her son well and did not believe any of his story. We expelled George from the school and district. I do not know what happened to him.

My principal arranged for a window to be cut into my office door. He was a smart leader who anticipated, and I needed my office to be visible in case kids continued to hit themselves on the table!

About thirty years later, I was the Principal at Watsonville High School, walking through a ceramics class. A young man was finishing the ceramic top of a bowl that he had just completed. The swirls of colors on the ceramic top were alluring and caused me to pause. I asked the student about his work, and he looked up at me, smiled wryly, pulled up the top, and said, "In here, Mr. Schekman, is a bowl of fuck you."

Years ago, I would not have asked about the underlying issues that this young man was facing. I certainly did not wonder about George's underlying issues about burning down a bathroom at the age of 13. But there were issues - poverty, no father in the house, gang influence….and the list goes on. The young man who had a bowl of fuck you was handled differently. I didn't take it personally and let him know his artwork was stellar and hoped that his day was okay. I went right to his counselor, and she followed up immediately. His grandmother died two days before, and he loved her and was hurting. Thirty years ago, I would've suspended that young man for his defiant and disruptive behavior. How stupid was that?

While George was burning bathrooms, other students were being "negatively reinforced" using corporal punishment, AKA paddling! The principal tasked me with supervising the process and coming back to him with a recommendation – do we keep the process, or do we stop beating the kids!?

I observed the other assistant principal one day set up the office environment to bring in a young man for paddling. The young man, Frank or Pollito, his street name, came in escorted by the assistant principal. Frank was smiling, surly, and showing no regard or respect for the assistant principal. The assistant principal, on the other hand, was visibly upset, veins showing in his neck and his face flustered red. He had cleared the office out, brought Frank into his office, and I served as a witness. He directed Frank to turn around and put his hands on the desk, bending over slightly. Frank was still laughing and challenging the assistant principal. The AP took the paddle, reached far back for a solid swing, and let it rip. The loud thwack could be heard outside of the office. It was awful. Frank was no longer laughing! He was upset, not crying but very red faced, anger showing in his eyes and his clenched fists. But then I looked at the AP and noticed that he was no longer angry. He was fine. He was content. He reached out to shake Frank's hands. "No hard feelings, Pollito," he said. I didn't realize it back then, but I needed to look at the underlying motivations of the adults around me! Frank, with his street name of Pollito, was already "gang influenced." He was a low reader, still transitioning from Spanish to English, not successful academically but found success with his friends. His father was absent from the picture, and his mother consented to the paddling, for she didn't know what to do and had faith in the schools. The principal and I agreed that paddling would stop! That was the last time any student was paddled at that middle school, to the best of my knowledge! California banned corporal punishment just a few years later, in 1986.

Dr. Jeffrey M. R. Duncan-Andrade is a professor of Latina/o Studies and Race and Resistance Studies at San Francisco State University. My school district had the good fortune of having Dr. Duncan-Andrade present directly to all 750 secondary teachers in the district. He also provided time to our future school-based counselors by presenting to my Counselor Ed classes at SJSU. His focus on trauma's impact on the brain shows the commonality between the traumas that kids experience in violent situations with our soldiers returning from our recent wars.

His article and lecture at Harvard – *"Note to Educators: Hope Required When Growing Roses in Concrete"* are profound in their impact on schools in California. Trauma-informed policies, trauma-informed instruction, and restorative practices started to take shape. It's never enough, but Duncan Andrade's outrage over the expectation that a kid is to take a standardized test after his brother was shot courses through my veins, thinking of how Pollito was paddled. That was all about expedience and ensuring that the adult's feelings were honored. I encourage you to read Duncan-Andrade's literature/research.

Go to YouTube
(https://www.youtube.com/watch?v=cWDh65ff8ss&t=1613s) and enjoy and learn from his presentation at Harvard. * Be prepared to hear a few expletives but he does apologize to his mother during his presentation. Duncan- Andrade's research is compelling, but his enthusiasm matches his research outcomes and makes his presentations even more worthwhile![vi]

****

Experience is such a wonderful commodity, and I recall

Andrade's comments to the faculty in my district on how important it is for our new teachers to recognize and learn from the veterans. This appears to be a more natural outcome in the world of elementary and less so in the world of secondary. I can reflect on my growth and experience and am grateful for my many teachers/mentors over the course of my career. But nothing matches real experiences.

Not too long ago, I appeared to have someone following me around Costco. That someone turned out to be Elias Gonzales, a former student of mine at EA Hall Middle School during the early 1990's. He graduated from Watsonville High School in 1995.

He followed me one day for he wasn't sure it was his former principal. But we stopped and checked in, had a pleasant walk down memory lane, caught up on his life, and he reminded me of a one-on-one basketball game way back when. He was in 8th grade, and I was his principal. He was a very cocky young man who let me know he could beat me one-on-one in basketball. We set up the game in front of 300 students, and I beat him soundly. He was embarrassed, but he let me know it was a great lesson and that the lesson in humility helped him come down to earth and provided him with an improved perspective. We agreed to sit down for coffee and check in with some more time and depth.

Elias is 45 years old and was expelled from high school but came

back and graduated from the school that expelled him-
Watsonville High School. He then attended Cabrillo College
and Cal State CSUMB, where he earned his Bachelor's. He is
now serving in a management position for the non-profit
MILPAS, an organization dedicated to the economic and
cultural enhancement of formerly incarcerated individuals and
other folks who represent the most needy and vulnerable in our
community. Sometimes, they provide resources/connections for
food, housing, and other support services, including counseling.
(For more info, go to https://milpacollective.org/)

Elias was late for our coffee for he approached two homeless
individuals near our meeting place and provided info,
encouragement, and his card. Of course, we talked about that
basketball game, and he reminded me of the great lesson I
provided. I had to confess to him that I was young and probably
was equally motivated by beating him than teaching him a
lesson. We were both cocky at that age. We laughed and he
reminded me of the greater lesson. He let me know that the "men
in my life left me, Mr. Schekman." He named a few male
teachers at Watsonville High who were there for him and
included me in that mix. I cried a bit and he then added that I
should've let him score a few points in that game. Apparently,
I "skunked" him. I should've looked for the underlying reasons
in his life and let him score some points! Experience, again, is

that most wonderful commodity. He survived and indicated that he learned a valuable life lesson.

Now, Elias is offering his wisdom and experience to our many needy folks in the Pàjaro Valley. It was an honor to hear his story and see what he is doing in life. My time with Elias reminded me of the incredible value of experience.

Elementary schools have the value of experience built into the systems, and much less so in our secondary schools. As the Interim Superintendent this past year, I spent more time in our elementary schools than in our secondary schools. My background is all secondary, and I wanted to learn more about learning in our elementary schools. I learned that new teachers must go out of their way to not get supported by the veterans. The veterans have more incentive to provide leadership because they receive each other's students and enjoy the benefit of effective teaching…. or not! Elementary children, simply put, provide more affection and love to their teachers, principals, and other staff. This developmental trait enhances the culture. Certainly, this is a generalization that is not always true.

Now our secondary schools are not all built to keep teachers and kids in silos. But without the right leadership in a school or a district, our secondary schools will "default" to teachers alone in a classroom with less contact with their peers. This is compared to an elementary program where there is a balance between the discussion of kids' progress and the curriculum. When secondary teachers are left alone in their classrooms, the system does not afford them time to share ideas about their kids' progress or lack of.

At Elias' school at that time, a large contingent of teachers wanted change. They were frustrated with the level of learning, low achieving outcomes and discipline. The focus on discipline has a long history at that school (and other schools, too!). It's my experience that discussion deals too much with the symptoms, not the problem. The work, planning, and discussions need to be on to be on the school-wide culture, and that focus needs to emphasize the positive. The kids and I were lucky at that time to have a faculty and staff work toward change that improved student learning! The school culture was generally positive, but the structure was not working.

Students were in a two-period Language Arts core one semester of science, and one of social studies. They also had PE and an elective. We changed the core to integrate Language Arts and Social Studies and afford the students a full year of science. However, the real power of our work was seen in the move toward interdisciplinary teams. Four teachers taught to a common group of students and, for the most part, had a common prep period. The master schedule design and placement of students were much more difficult to achieve. The discussions between teachers were much more about the students who were not successful.

Many of the "unsuccessful" students were successful in some of their classes, and the teachers could learn from each other about what works. THE TEACHERS HAD PLANNING AND COLLABORATIVE TIME BUILT INTO THEIR WORK SCHEDULE. This is important in secondary schools and makes an immediate difference in student behavior. Four teachers could intervene with a family, and they were on the same page. Counselors coordinated their support through the interdisciplinary teams, and our support for struggling students was more targeted and effective. The school implemented rewards and recognition SYSTEMS to help all staff focus on the positive. One idea that came to fruition is the Flying Falcon! These were slips of paper that any adult on campus could hand over to a student doing anything positive! There was a raffle at the end of the week with prizes and names announced over the loudspeaker- a simple idea with a good impact on students AND staff. That concept of everyone being on the same page was paying off. We shared a common vision and the pathway to the academic outcomes for our students.

Organizing the school into interdisciplinary teams clearly was a step in the right direction with regard to student learning. Inheriting a solid faculty is not always in the cards when a new principal is hired. But our kids, their families, and I were lucky! I learned from a veteran and caring faculty. They wanted change and worked with the admin and each other to effect change. We had 3 of Howard's characteristics in place but were lacking the explicit acknowledgment of race and intensive academic interventions. This was the bigger context for Elias in his middle school. But I should have let him score some points! Sorry, Elias!

*****

I left that fine middle school as the Assistant Principal in 1984 and came back 6 years later to serve as Principal. I left in 1994 to open a new high school in Salinas, California, 23 miles down the road. Opening a new high school was my dream since I worked at the new high school in Castroville with my most important mentor. Opening a new high school generally means that one gets to hire all staff and build a school culture from scratch- an exciting concept for a young and aspiring administrator! I was honored! But I also recognized again that timing in hiring for leadership positions in schools is critical. I got lucky.

The politics of the board at that time was such that they were going to hire an outsider. There were many highly capable individuals in the district who would've done an excellent job at the new high school. The quotes in the press were "the district needed a fresh perspective…"!

I did get to hire some excellent classified and certificated staff for the opening of Everett Alvarez High School in August of 1995. Everett Alvarez Jr. was a navy pilot shot down in Vietnam during the war. He spent time in the "Hanoi Hilton" with John McCain, the late Senator from Arizona. Having a living and breathing hero serve as our namesake helped us build the school culture. His book "Chained Eagle" motivated the students, parents, and staff to choose the eagle as the mascot. His lessons about honor, character, and country were helpful in laying the foundation for our developing school culture. The gold and blue colors also came from the navy. He presented at the opening ceremony, the first commencement ceremony, and on many other occasions. In every one of his presentations, he helped to define the developing school culture and showed a great deal of enthusiasm for our students and the community!

On the opening day of Everett Alvarez High School, August 25, 1995, I handed my camcorder over to our Athletic Director and asked him to walk around the campus and video whatever he felt was worthwhile. It was history in the making on the first day of the new high school!!!!! The kids, staff, parents, and community were excited. I took my camcorder home and shared it with my young family!

Unfortunately, my very young children witnessed seven fights on the video. Yes, there were seven fights on our first day of classes!!!! We had lots of work and learning in front of us! The north part of the town, known as Santa Rita, had not mingled with the kids from East Salinas in their travels through the world of K-8! We needed to act to create a culture that did the opposite of leading to fights. And we did!

What makes a positive school culture? According to Leah Shafer in the Harvard Graduate School of Education publication, July of 2018 – "It starts with connections — strong and overlapping interactions among all members of the school community."vii

So, how does one build those connections in a new school when all the employees are new to the site and most of them are new to each other? It was a challenge to build that culture, but the community of Salinas embraced its newest high school both with support and reasonable ideas about how the school culture should look and feel.

With seven fights on that first day, the staff knew we had some work to do related to our school-wide culture. Let me introduce Lori Villanueva. At that time, she served as a science teacher at EAHS. She announced to the staff that she was dealing with too much rude behavior at the school. She organized a spaghetti luncheon and invited 25 students and 10 adults from the campus, including me.

We had a good time, talked about etiquette and manners, and brainstormed ways to improve the school culture. I wasn't sure how a spaghetti luncheon would spur us on to an improved culture and climate, but I enjoyed the moment of positive energy and discussion with our staff and the good food, too! Lori went on to serve as an Assistant Principal in the district and then as a middle school principal. She is presently the Superintendent of Schools in the Coalinga Huron School District.

One of our assistant principals attended the spaghetti luncheon and moved us forward by getting trained by the Josephson Institute on a character development program called Character Counts. Gina Muller worked with me as a counselor at my two previous assignments and provided strong leadership with the implementation of Character Counts to help move our school wide culture in a positive direction. The six pillars of Character Counts are:

- Trustworthiness

- Responsibility

- Respect

- Fairness

- Caring

- Citizenship

The program is set up so schools can use these six pillars to reinforce behavior in a variety of ways. This kind of flexibility allowed the staff to use its creative juices to apply the concepts in the classrooms and around the campus. We had a parent who was a professional photographer. She volunteered to take pictures of two students each month, frame and put the pictures under glass-a professional portrait. We dedicated one wall in the main office for the pictures to be displayed. The idea was that one female senior and one male senior would be selected as the "Character Counts Senior of the Month," and their portraits would then be prominently displayed in the main office. Over the course of the next few years that wall was adorned with our top students, but not an academic designation. I used to see some of the younger students come in and tell each other that they hoped to see themselves up on that wall. The faculty selected the two students each month based on the student's alignment with the six pillars! Certainly, there were other aspects of Character Counts that permeated the campus. School culture is created, maintained and improved by the adults involved with the school, on and off campus. It doesn't have to be Character Counts, but there does need to be clear intentionality of purpose, and again, everyone has to be on the same page!

There needs to be a positive approach in all aspects of building school culture. A focus on the outcomes of negative behavior, a common theme at our middle schools, is not the focus needed to address school culture! Even our phraseology, the words, signs, and symbols at a school represent the culture. NO STUDENTS ALLOWED on the faculty room door sends an important message. What about the FACULTY ROOM? Isn't that sufficient? Phrasing the positive outcomes of what is expected versus phrasing what our students can't do is a simple step forward.

More importantly, the behaviors of the adults toward the students and their families are the centerpiece of school culture.

Dr. Joyce Epstein, researcher and author, has some basic tenets that are foundational when assessing school culture[viii]:

- *Just about all families care about their children*

- *Just about all administrators and teachers say they want to involve families*

- *Just about all students want their families to be knowledgeable partners in their schooling!*

Opening a new high school and having the year before to get ready meant that the school had a chance to implement these basic tenets of Dr. Epstein. We had some successes and enough less-than-successful outcomes. Everett Alvarez High School opened in 1995 with 9th and 10th-grade students. We were blessed with a good staff and an eager group of students and parents. We grew each year, adding a grade level, and thus the culture changed. But, working to put systems in place while the school was smaller appeared to be a good idea. Our Community Liaison, Sandra Cervantes, was from the community of Salinas and had excellent experience at one of the district middle schools. Her passion, dedication, and communication skills made things happen. She trained 20 to 30 parents each year to make phone calls to other parents. Twice a month, 20 parents would come into our admin and counseling offices at 5:00 pm and begin making calls to parents about upcoming meetings and events. This personal touch made a huge difference and led to large turnouts of parents at important meetings. I recall that we had to move an English Language Advisory Council meeting from the library to the gym for 800 parents who showed up! In my previous sites, we had 30 or so parents attend this function. Part of it was the excitement at the new school, but most of it was our outreach and responsiveness to our community. Almost the entire staff was on the same page those first years, and our enthusiasm was well represented in the classrooms, on the sporting fields, and in the community.

Ms. Cervantes left after three years, and we didn't have the turnout that we had when Sandra worked as our Community Liaison. We used Epstein's three points and did well with our parental awareness and involvement, for we kept receiving student transfers from the other schools, a sign of some of our successful work and the perception in the community. Sandra had a personal connection with our parents. She also provided hope for our parents who struggled with the high school systems, and she always did her job with enthusiasm! She had the ganas to help our parents help their kids. It's the system that we plan for and utilize, but when a school employee shows the kind of enthusiasm, dedication, and compassion that Ms. Cervantes did, the outcomes are better!

Everett Alvarez HS had its first senior class in 1998! That year, the school agreed to host an event entitled "Every Fifteen Minutes." It was a cooperative effort by the police and fire departments in advance of the high school proms, a psychodrama showing a horrific car accident with students getting killed. Students served as actors, and the police department left a crushed car in the middle of the campus. One student thespian did an excellent job of makeup, and our "dead" students spilled out of the car, looking gruesome and dead. We only allowed juniors and seniors to participate. The school staff even called the parents of the "dead" students to inform them of their son/daughter being killed. (The parents knew in advance.) They came to the school, and we put the kids' bodies in body bags. I was impressed that everyone was taking this psychodrama very seriously. No one was laughing and we had a crowd of 700 teenagers. The drama worked.

We went into the gymnasium for some planned presentations. The parents also joined us. Some of the students, parents, AND staff started to cry. I was unprepared! None of us were prepared! One of our seniors came to the mike and started bawling. He apologized to his family, especially his father. His father then came up and also apologized to his son and family. Others came to the microphone and also apologized. Some shared family secrets! It was an incredible moment filled with grief and sadness! The kids, families, and some of the staff were overwhelmed with emotion, and the gymnasium, even though it was filled with people, apparently served as a safe place to express their sorrow and grief!

Unfortunately, we were not prepared for this outpouring. We used an organization called Grief Busters to provide additional support and counseling if there was a tragedy in the community. But, we did not plan for any additional support following the psychodrama. The learning for the staff (and me) was simple. So many of our young folks live in a world of trauma, poverty, violence, and single-parent families! (And this was before the birth of social media, so we now know how social media intensifies the negative for teens and tweens! The Surgeon General is now wanting to put warning labels on social media apps!) Even the vision of the tragedy of a horrific auto accident was enough to trigger so much emotion. Had we been prepared, we would have had rooms available for crying kids and adults. We would have brought Grief Busters on the campus, but we did not anticipate this kind of emotional fallout. Anticipation!

I was Principal at Everett Alvarez from 1994 through June of 2001. During that time, our school's community lost six young men to violence. Five of them had claimed some sort of gang affiliation, and one was hitting on the girl of an affiliate and was shot. None of the violence was on campus but was brought to the campus by others. Retribution was something we did need to anticipate. Our Campus Supervisors, very connected to the community, would let me know the background of a shooting. If a blue was shot, we'd ready ourselves for them to respond! If a red was shot, the same readiness level was needed.

In the second year of EAHS gang activity in town heightened and on campus. At one point, we ALLOWED gang affiliates to designate "their" area. It made it easier for our supervision, but it was so WRONG! An educational liaison from the ag company Tanimura and Antle (TNA) chastised me for this tacit acceptance of those designated areas. It gave those students, a small minority, power for the wrong reason. Other students, non-gang-affiliated students, were intimidated and not able to feel safe and comfortable in either of those areas.

TNA is an example of a progressive company interested in hiring graduates from our community. Watsonville, like all communities, also has companies hoping to hire graduates from the local schools. But too often, our students' readiness skills, including soft skills, were not at the readiness level. Everett Alvarez developed partnerships with non-profit agencies and companies like TNA, and we then were open to their help and their criticism. Cheryl Ward Kaiser was that representative from TNA. She could be highly critical of our practices, and she was usually right. But we listened. Our test scores went down one year, and she let me have it! "The new high school's scores go down?!" They went up the next year and steadily after that. TNA helped the school open its first California Partnership Academy and purchased a new pick-up truck for the International Agribusiness Academy.

That program is still flourishing. TNA and other companies are able to hire students from that academy who graduate from the local high schools and continue their studies at Hartnell, Cal Poly San Luis Obispo, Fresno State, UC Davis, and more. California Partnership Academies offers academics and integrates important career themes to help develop specific skills, including those important soft skills – communication in writing and in person, punctuality, collegiality, good work ethic, and more! The openness of the school culture afforded our kids and staff opportunities to connect with and get support from a plethora of wonderful problem solvers in the community. The community has its problems, as do all, but opening a new high school in Salinas was an honor, for there are so many generous individuals who work to resolve those problems.

Burnout set in, and I left EAHS after 7 years. A good foundation was built, and the school enjoyed a positive image in the community, and there was a commonality of purpose and a sense of togetherness on the staff. For the most part, we were on the same page…and yes, the test scores went up! Opening a new school has the advantage of hiring staff with a commonality of purpose. We hired a balance of teachers from the district's high schools and middle schools. Most were mavericks who were unhappy with the present status quo of public-school education and wanted to see change on behalf of ALL KIDS' learning. It took a longer time to move forward with so many strong-willed individuals but a very positive school culture grew and four specific strategies stand out:

1. Strong connections with the community. This was true of our parent community, the faith community, post-secondary schools, and businesses; large and small.

2. Relevant and meaningful lessons in all classes with the expectation that all kids can learn, and all kids deserve the chance to choose college after high school.

3. Beginning wherever possible interdisciplinary themes-the International Agribusiness Academy was the first example.

4. Strong counseling support

My wife and family were instrumental in helping me with my career and my stress. My kids were young. I needed more time with my family and wanted a change. I then became the Director of Pupil Personnel Services in the district, which included serving as Principal of Mt. Toro Continuation High School and overseeing the expulsion process. I didn't have the benefit of Jeff Duncan Andrade's research on trauma and the brain when I took this job, but I learned very quickly about the concept of HOPE! We had students in the world of alternative ed. who had no hope for their future.

Some saw their futures in prison. Some saw their futures in a lucrative drug dealing business, and there were some students who recognized their own issues and worked hard to get back in the groove of their education. Again, we had the support of many support services in the community. Our Teen Parent program was a model program, and young teen mothers who were at risk in other school environments represented the top tier of success at Mt. Toro. The school needed to focus on skill building, but it was more important to help students have hope for their future. Duncan Andrade challenged his audience at Harvard about the importance of taking standardized tests while students are grieving over the deaths of their friends, family, and neighbors! The students in the world of alternative ed. had to deal with all sorts of obstacles and impediments to their learning. Our program helped students become successful in increments. They would see each credit that they earned, one credit at a time. Students often would earn their diploma before their peers back at the comprehensive high school they came from. When a student met the graduation requirements, I would get on the PA and announce their name, and the school would celebrate that student's success at that moment in time. The graduate and I would take a Polaroid photo and post the photo in the office. More pictures would adorn the office as the year progressed. This kind of recognition is obviously honoring our graduates, but it also is a simple way of providing hope for the other students and adding to the school culture.

Two short anecdotes – We had a student from Los Angeles who was so hardened from the streets the adults, including me, had a hard time understanding the words that he spoke. Our school was neutral, although some neighborhoods in Salinas were not! We did a good job of supervising and had a very positive school culture on behalf of our students' learning. But this young man had no hope. He had three "almost" fights by 10:00 am on his first day. He charged one of our more buff teachers, and that was the end of this young man's tenure at Mt. Toro. We were not equipped to help a young man who was so devoid of hope.

On another day, we brought a DJ to the school to simply enjoy the lunchtime environment. He obviously played their music, and I noticed four young ladies tapping their toes. I encouraged them to get up and dance, and they all asked me in unison, "How many credits?" I wondered if our credit-in-increment system began to surpass the importance of learning!

During my four years in the world of alt ed I was able to see students come in the front door discouraged and limited with their hope. Most students, in the beginning, expressed their goal to return to their comprehensive high school.

Very few returned, not a bad thing! They were successful at Mt. Toro, and success begets success! The graduates and their families were honored at their commencement with great aplomb. The enthusiasm shown by the graduates, families, staff, and members of the community was as strong as any other commencement I've attended. I learned more from our alternative ed students than they learned from me!

Culture can be felt at the district level, starting with the Board and the Superintendent. Do the practices encourage a focus on learning? Are policies inclusive? Is the board responsive to the community? The Pàjaro Valley USD saw the Migrant Education diminish in numbers because of a change in population and more restrictive state requirements. The director of the program worked diligently to develop leadership among the migrant population and pushed hard back against some of the state's efforts, for he saw kids and families losing services. He also led an event every year that highlighted the graduating migrant ed students. It was more than a simple recognition ceremony. The Mello Center for Performing Arts, with a capacity of 750 students, would be filled to capacity to honor 15-20 students. The grads would be on the stage, and their stories would be highlighted in words and pictures. The difference between this event and other similar celebrations is that the leaders in our town and county were present. It was more of a celebration of their brilliant futures versus the highlighting of the obstacles leading to this point. He would always finish by saying the name of the student and "Es el rostro del Programa de Educación Migrante!" The student is the face of the Migrant Education Program. His inflection, tone, and **enthusiasm** with that sentence moved the audience each time. His daily work with his students and community also led to these kinds of successes. This kind of work had positive effects on the district's work in the community, something I got to see upon my return to the PVUSD. It's all about leadership!

I didn't forget his name! He left that position to serve as Assistant Superintendent in Monterey and then Santa Cruz

County. He presently serves as the Superintendent of Schools for Santa Cruz County, and his name is Dr. Faris Sabbah!

Another example of enthusiastic leadership led to a positive school culture with a strong emphasis on parental involvement. The first time I met Casey O'Brien, he was serving as an Assistant Principal at EA Hall Middle School. He came to my son's elementary school to talk with the 5th graders and their families. He was so happy to meet the families and so proud of what the school was achieving. His words were as meaningful to the parents, and his tone was supportive. He was sincere and more than enthused. We were all made to feel welcome, even with his broken Spanish! He made us feel a part of the process and that our kids were heading into a great adventure. My son ended up at a different middle school but Mr. O'Brien became Principal at that school. A few years later, he became the Principal of Aptos High School and helped improve the school culture at that school. I observed him participating in a tricycle race with the students at that high school. As he headed down the hill, he would literally kick students out of the way. He was also very competitive, and the kids and parents loved him.

Jacob, my son, was a 7th grader at Lakeview Middle School. He was a good student and enjoyed school. I worked in a different district in Salinas, but Jacob's mother, my wife, worked at the school. What a support system! We learned that his math teacher gave out worksheets every day and had the students work quietly and independently on each of the sheets. We were concerned about her "methodology". Our son then informed us that when he needed help, he'd approach her desk, and she'd hold up a STOP SIGN and tell him to sit down, another crappy aspect of her methodology.

Mr. O'Brien was aware of her ineffective teaching for he was visible on his campus and in the classrooms. I set up a meeting with the teacher to question her practices and Mr. O'Brien joined us. Remember, I'm a parent in this situation.

The teacher's defensiveness showed up even before I got to my concern about the stop sign. She let us know her qualifications and history of recognition. I asked her about her stop sign, and she burst into tears. She started yelling that she was being ganged up by school administrators. She ran out of the room leaving Casey and I sitting there to wonder about our next steps-his as the administration and mine as a parent. Our next steps became a moot point. That teacher did not show up the next day or for the rest of the year. A long-term sub came in, and that teacher resigned. Part of that process was the principal's high visibility in the classrooms for the teacher knew that her principal was aware of the ineffectiveness of her teaching. His enthusiasm was a factor in improving the overall culture at Lakeview Middle School, and his classroom walk-throughs kept the focus on student learning!

Mr. O'Brien went on to serve as Principal of Aptos High and is presently the Director of Student Services in Santa Cruz. His enthusiasm and influence are felt at the district level.

Making a Full Circle

Watsonville High School, established in 1892, was central to my career and my family. My three children attended, and my wife and all her siblings also graduated from WHS. I started teaching in 1975 as a long-term substitute teacher there and was able to stay the entire year, for the teacher I replaced couldn't return that year due to health issues. I LOVED EVERY MINUTE OF THAT JOB. I taught Algebra and Geometry. The Department Chair tried to hire me, but I wasn't credentialed for math and my Spanish was still in need of improving! However, I came back twice, ten years later as an assistant principal and then twenty years later as the principal. I went from one of the newest schools in the Monterey Bay area to one of the oldest. Finally, last year, as the Interim Superintendent, Watsonville High received a fair amount of my attention!

The year prior to coming to Watsonville High, I was not in the district but lived six blocks from Watsonville High. I was aware of the incredible difficulties going on at the campus. Teachers were upset with each other and with the administration. The admin had a small following trying to establish smaller learning communities, which is a good idea. But there was too much infighting with the staff, and unity appeared to be impossible. The Union President set up shop at the site, as did the Board

President, a former teacher at that high school, and former Union President. Role confusion. This was our middle child's senior year at WHS. I attended the graduation ceremony and saw students together with each other and blow-up dolls, clearly not caring about the speakers on the stage until one graduate started playing his guitar. I always believe that a spirited and positive graduation ceremony is the culmination of four years of work. That ceremony in 2005 was a sad representation of the school culture and the feeling tone of the graduates.

But their families were proud, and the Class of 2005 moved on. I left there a bit sad.

Little did I know that I would end up as the principal of that wild and crazy place NEXT YEAR!

Yes, I returned to my beloved WHS, knowing that there were major issues.

- Very low test scores

- Unfriendly school environment

- Divided faculty

- At least 20 out of 80 teachers were ineffective

- Facility and grounds in bad shape

I didn't know I would be there, but I made this journey with my

9th grade son, for he entered at the same time I did, giving me a sentimental journey into what was my final principal-ship, sentimental but absolutely the most challenging job of my career.

While working in my former district the site administrators went through a very thorough training with Robert Marzano. His research enhanced my walkthroughs in the classrooms. I was always a hyper principal and visited all the classrooms regularly, but Marzano's "Characteristics of the Effective Classroom" enhanced my knowledge and application. The teachers at WHS were not used to the principal visiting so frequently, and many were suspicious. Near the end of my first year, a very upbeat art teacher asked me if she was doing something wrong because I had been in her class so often. I responded that I've been in everyone's classroom the same amount of time. Her eyes widened, "Then you know where all of the skeletons are!" What she meant is that everyone at the site knew-there were a lot of ineffective teachers! The level of engagement in some of our classes was in the negative. One teacher made deals with his students related to their cell phones. If the admin came in and took their phone, it was on them. They would have to say that the teacher did not allow it! His content wasn't delivered, but he was adept at teaching cynicism!

The previous year was so divisive that over $1,000,000 in categorical funds were left over and had to be spent before April

1! Crazy! Those funds were for a targeted population in the previous few years. We upgraded the computer labs and bought lots of pizza!!!!! (Say what? Pizza? Stay tuned for the significance!)

My administration attacked the low-test scores in several ways. We showed the last 10 years of WHS test scores comparing it to a high school down the road with 3 times the number of English Learners. Our scores were identical, yet WHS had only 700 English Learners, and the other school had 1800. The staff looked at the scores and did reflect in a good way, well most of them. One teacher told the staff that we were racist if we kept going in that direction. I sensed some movement, but there were still those 20 very weak teachers who would only negatively impact our efforts and, with their ineffective pedagogy, negatively impact our kids' learning and, ultimately, the test scores.

So, that's where the pizza came in. I believe that a school culture should help young people develop an intrinsic sense of motivation, but we were in a difficult bind, so we focused on bribery! We did not just hand over pizza to the kids during the testing. We began a phone campaign to personally invite the police chief, the mayor, city council members, county supervisors, and many wonderful leaders in our community to come serve the pizza to the kids on the day of testing. We had

6 days of testing over a two-week period. We set up fifty stations around campus for the pizza to be handed out. During the testing, the teachers served as proctors. They handed a ticket to each student who made an effort on the test. The year before, there was no concerted effort by the staff or students, and it showed. But this year, the students were told that if they tried, they would get a slice of pizza immediately after the test. I cannot forget the most important part of that process. Every one of our volunteers knew the right words to say to the students as they handed over the pizza. "Thanks for trying. We're proud of you." The students saw the Watsonville Police Chief, the Mayor, and so many others on campus thanking them and congratulating them. The kids felt important, and one unanticipated outcome included the many adults on campus letting me know, "How nice the kids are here!" It was clear that too many folks in the town were not aware of the good work going on at WHS. That would also soon change! Our test results rose 39 points that year, the largest one-year rise in the school's history.

But staffing still was an issue at that school for too many teachers didn't care about kids' learning. This showed up first and foremost in the classroom but also at the many different meetings staff attended. It was a difficult place to bring people together with a common vision!!! However enough teachers did share a common vision about smaller learning communities. The school had three California Partnership Academies, Business, Tech, and Ag (BATA), the Video Academy, and the Medical Careers Academy. As ENOUGH teachers bought into the concept, the school grew four more academies – Environmental Science and Natural Resources (ESNER), Public and Community Services (ECHO-Police, fire, teaching, and service industry), Engineering and a Fine Arts Academy called MOSAIC. We applied for grants to the State of California, and lo and behold, we became what was called a "wall-to-wall" academy school. All kids had to make a choice as to which academy to go to in the 10th grade. The difficulty in designing and maintaining a master schedule that called for common preps and common students in key academic classes was a challenge, to say the least. The admin that came in after inherited those difficulties kept the vision intact and made the academies work!

We almost lost one academy due to the poor leadership in that academy. But a change in leadership and a plea to the state kept this academy in place and it is thriving to this day. But those many weak teachers kept the school from moving forward in a way that the community deserved. Our Chief Business Office at the time, Brett McFadden heard the pleas about a weak faculty and moved an early retirement package forward. Teachers could choose to retire early, begin their pension with the state, and collect $100,000.00 over a five-year period, $20,000.00 per year.

We lost a few excellent teachers in our district, but at my school, we witnessed the retirement of many who, simply put, needed to retire. Many were just burned out, having taught in one place for so many years. This plan saves the district over time, not immediately. Veteran teachers at the top of the salary table were generally replaced by newer teachers whose salaries were less.

Our CBO also worked diligently to help deal with the ongoing difficulties of maintaining and improving our aging facilities, and our newest high school needed and deserved a stadium and comprehensive athletic facility. We had gotten through the "Great Recession of 2008," but the conservative aura of no new taxes permeated our county, including some members of our board. Mr. McFadden plugged away. I took our conservative board member and had him tour our newest high school, Pajaro Valley HS, with students and staff. He came out of the tour wondering if he'd be considered a racist if we didn't move forward with a bond.

In the year 2012, the district passed a $150 million dollar bond that included a stadium for the newest high school. Mr. McFadden was clear with the vision about what the bond would do. He articulated that vision with the board and very actively in the community. He showed enthusiasm, expertise, and hope for the district's future. Now, 14 years later, the district is working toward passing a $315 million bond. Clearly, the state does not provide enough money for districts to do what is necessary to improve and maintain our aging buildings.

Mr. McFadden went on to serve as a superintendent and brought his creative expertise to other communities. But I have one more story to tell. Our teamwork helped the district in many ways. His willingness to learn about curricular and instructional issues brought the money guy into the planning and discussion related to many important areas for our classrooms-from technology to the implementation of the new science standards. One day, he was on the phone with a rather conservative member of our community who badgered our poor CBO to the point that Mr. McFadden suggested that our member of the community move to Idaho or another location where his beliefs are more accepted. That member of our community showed up to the public session of our next board meeting. It wasn't the first time that our superintendent took the CBO "behind the barn."

It's All About Leadership and I've been fortunate to have a few CBOs in my career who took an active pursuit in learning about curriculum and instruction. Their leadership clearly enhanced student learning for resources were then placed more strategically. Mr. McFadden would well represent John Lewis' "good trouble."

Watsonville High has a long history of success and failure, as do all schools, and was my greatest challenge in my career but we enjoyed so many success stories, sometimes in spite of ourselves.

One of my students grew up in a home with **alcohol**, abuse, and violence. She managed to transcend her circumstances and graduated from WHS in 2009.

Her attendance was awful; however, she was able to earn her credits and make progress toward graduation. During her senior year, she was recommended for placement at one of the alternative sites because of her attendance. Her mother appealed against the involuntary transfer, and she was given a second chance. She went on to graduate from the University of California, Santa Cruz, and worked for the Santa Cruz County Office of Education as an educator and counselor. She is still working in an outreach capacity with young people with a local government official. She is a superb model of brilliance and resilience for our young people today, and that second chance was clearly worth it. The school staff took the time to look at the underlying reasons, and she went on to help other young folks have a positive vision of their future.

A similar event happened in another school district when I received a call from Manuel Nuñez, then principal of a continuation school (and my student at SJSU!) He was frustrated because he inherited an attendance policy that kicked in an automatic removal from the site if student attendance was a problem. Manny (now Dr. Nuñez and Assistant Superintendent in charge of Human Resources in the Monterey Peninsula USD) had a female student who had similar familial experiences as the student at Watsonville High. Her attendance was slipping, and some of his staff expected him to kick her out. He called me very frustrated one day, and we brainstormed. I asked about her progress in her academics, and he knew she was doing well. He gave her that chance and she graduated from that high school but would not have had they adhered to the site's policy. Every situation is different but second chances, when planned and communicated, usually do pay off in the right way.

Getting Closure with WHS

However, I had one last lingering issue to grapple with – the wildness at the graduation ceremony. I met with our student leaders as the planning began. I asked for their kindness and respect during the ceremony. During my speech, I would pause for five minutes to let them do their thing. They appreciated the chance to provide their input, and it worked. We had a GREAT ceremony. They let the silly string, tortillas, and beach balls fly at the right part of the commencement. I was proud of them, and it was not academic, but it was about school culture, and again, the answer was right there in front of me. In my time as a high school principal, I would work hard to get the juniors there to attend! Their presence added to the ceremony and readied them for next year's ceremony!

The same four strategies from my time at Everett Alvarez High School were incorporated at Watsonville High. The circumstances were different, but we also enjoyed positive outcomes!

1. Strong connections with the community. We did this to enhance our testing environment and motivating our students. Each academy, new and established, needed a community advisory board representing the career

path…and it began with the serving of pizza!

2. Relevant and meaningful lessons in all classes with the expectation that all kids can learn, and all kids deserve the chance to choose college after high school. (Sounds like EAHS!) This was done with purposeful staff development and the early retirement of 20 teachers from WHS!

3. Beginning wherever possible interdisciplinary themes-Three academies were already in place and four more were added through successful grant writing and community connections.

4. Strong counseling support. This was already in place at WHS, but the counselors' leadership was critical to the changes being implemented at WHS.

5. Commonality of Purpose- Not everyone but most the staff came together. That pizza year saw a 39-point growth in the achievement. That, combined with the advent of four new academies created some momentum to continue to move forward.

Building and Sustaining Leadership

We need to include some key groups to run our schools. It does not happen automatically, but leaders who are inclusive of key groups on and off campus are going to be more effective in meeting important goals. If that inclusiveness is the result of the union's pressures, either classified or certificated, then discussion and planning will take place. But if the inclusion of these key groups is because of the leadership's invitations and initiatives, progress will be enhanced. Systemizing inclusivity is the goal! One can see it in the school culture!!!!

The Classified Staff are the bloodlines of any school or any school district. They are underpaid in almost all cases. In my last district, some of our classified staff stayed in place because of the excellent medical benefits. Indeed, some of their salaries were less than the district's cost for health benefits! This one issue will implode in the next few years!

Too often, we do not include our classified staff as thought partners and collaborators in the planning of our programs and systems. It is easy to gauge the effectiveness of site and district leadership by surveying the classified staff. Accreditation review committees work to include the classified staff. Several years ago, the President of the local Classified School

Employees Association (CSEA) held up her keys to the auditorium filled with employees of the Salinas Union HSD. "We have the keys," she reiterated with enthusiasm. "We let folks in the door or not!" The brainpower that I have been afforded by the classified staff members has been invaluable. Our bus drivers helped with the reduction of routes. Our classified food services employees are working to bring better quality food to our children. I see more and more healthy food as I visit our K-12 schools. The classified staff are an overlooked gift, and we need to make sure that they are included.

During my visits to the sites last year as the Interim Superintendent, every elementary school office enjoyed the welcomes and pleasantries of two classified employees, usually the Office Manager and the Office Assistant. They set the tone for the school every day. On one occasion, I visited an elementary site with the admin home sick and the office manager handling the discipline! She was stressed and on the phone with a parent but kept it going. She kept herself upbeat, and yes, I stayed and helped with the discipline! Parents came and picked up their children, and the crunch was over. I will never forget her willingness to keep school going! Her leadership was more than needed. She knew the impact on the campus and took charge. I left, asking her when she would go back to school to earn her teaching credential. I am proud to say that there are at least five teachers out there in my past who started in the classified ranks and were invited to consider teaching!

The other group that needs to be included in leadership decisions at the school site is the counselors. Wingfield, Reese, and West-Olatunji[ix] show that the culture of a school is enhanced when counselors are involved in leadership decisions.

Counselors have a unique set of skills to help stay in touch with our students and parents and provide that pulse to leaders on campus, in the district, and in the community. I found out early in my career how impactful an ineffective counselor was and know the inverse is true. Universities are working hard to keep up with the real world of training counselors for the challenging world of K-12. I had the pleasure of teaching a diverse group of graduate students at SJSU and then placing them as Counseling Interns in many districts on the central coast of California. It was a delight to visit them as interns and then see them hired! Several of my counseling graduates made the natural switch from counseling to school administration. Counselors' roles need to expand beyond their offices. Simple examples include the School Site Council, the Leadership "Cabinet" at the site, parent informational meetings, and more.

Parents are the other key group where leadership can and should be facilitated. Counselors know how to help parents understand the underlying issues with their children. Some parents come through the front door of the school, know how to help their own children, and can offer their services to support the school in a variety of ways. Other parents want to help but do not have the wherewithal, and some parents are in dysfunctional relationships and we in schools need to understand and connect those families with levels of support from the district and the community. I was part of a program in Salinas entitled Families in Control. Parents who were struggling with their teens would be part of a training program with their teens that helped them with strategies of communication and developing intrinsic motivation. We placed families in the program in lieu of the suspension of their child. I was part of a process that worked with those underlying reasons, and it helped those families.

As I pursue some closure here, I want to share specific strategies that were discussed in the article. I also wish to highlight these specific strategies and the researchers behind them. While many decisions made by school leaders are situational, there are fundamental ideas that consistently work. I had the opportunity to see them in action even before fully understanding the academic concepts behind them!

Highlighting Specific Strategies

1. **Involving Counselors in Leadership Positions** – When counselors play leadership roles in school, the focus shifts more towards the entire child! Their leadership can

contribute in various ways, all benefiting the ever-evolving culture of a school!

2. **School Culture** – Dr. Epstein's three basic tenets of building school culture serve as an excellent point of departure for all schools!

- *Just about all families care about their children*

- *Just about all administrators and teachers say they want to involve families*

- *Just about all students want their families to be knowledgeable* partners about their schooling!

3. **Trauma-Informed Instruction** – Designing lessons, as well as school and district policies, with trauma-informed instruction, will enhance individual learning and school culture. Duncan-Andrade's research is meaningful from the classroom to every other area of a student's upbringing. If a student is not learning, the first question to ask is: What are the underlying reasons? This question is particularly important when addressing student absenteeism.

4. **Connections Within the School Community** – Habib's and Colannino's work demonstrates that connections among staff, students, parents, and community partners are vital for a school's success.

5. **Structuring Secondary Schools** – Secondary schools should organize the master schedule of classes to provide teachers with common preparation time and, whenever possible, offer the same benefit to students. Sharing successful instructional strategies along with student achievement data is always helpful for our classroom teachers. They are the experts. It is important, though less common, for teachers to share their ideas about students who are struggling so that they can improve where they are lacking. Interdisciplinary teams, partnership academies, collaborative projects, and these kinds of structures enhance student learning.

6. **Community Engagement** – All schools need to establish strong communication and connections within the community. Leah Shafer's research shows us that strong community connection ties enhance school culture. It wasn't the pizza that resonated with the students in the long run. It was the message from our community's leaders – "Thanks for trying!" That message also reinforced the good work of the teachers!

7. **Teaching Leadership Early** – Teaching leadership in the elementary years fosters good leadership as students move on to middle and high schools. The answers to many of the common problems are found within the student body, where

creativity is often undervalued. We need to structure our schools to honor students' input and ideas. The same concept applies to our parents! We have to seek input and be ready to listen to the concerns!

8. **Commonality of Purpose** – Numerous researchers have emphasized the importance of this basic tenet. The process of achieving it, however, is where one's leadership skills are truly tested! Bringing people together is both a science and an art!

Summarizing – Finally!!!!

The extreme conservative wing at the national level has negatively influenced local politics. Fear, anger, and false narratives have replaced the notion of integrity, moderation, transparency, and respect in addressing important issues. The Ethnic Studies requirement in the State of California is an attempt to be inclusive and provide REAL and ACCURATE information about the events in our history, both positive and negative! Unfortunately, the discussion in too many districts is not about the teaching or the content, but it is about vague "culture wars" that distract from our children's learning. I want to advocate for positive change so that our local democracies can again represent their communities and focus on the issues of improving our children's learning. The overt negativity of these "discussions" takes the governing board's attention away from the real policy discussions that support the improvement and enhancement of student's learning. It also dampens the enthusiasm of the community at a time when we need our communities to understand the issues that our educators and parents face in our K-12 schools at this time.

Why the Underlying Theme
Here is Enthusiasm!!!

I attended my son's commencement at the University of Southern Mississippi, where he earned his Ph.D. in Polymer Science and Engineering! Of course, I was as happy as I could be when they announced his name. As he walked across the stage and paused, the Department Chair adorned him with his sash/hood. I felt immense pride. But something else happened - I realized that as other families cheered for their children, I found myself applauding their children as well if their cheering was close to where I was seated. Their enthusiasm, simply put, was contagious. Others shared their pride and joy in the room. We all had that pleasure and contentment in common, whether it was a child, grandchild, sibling, spouse, or friend who walked across that stage to receive their degree.

Enthusiasm is the central theme of what I am pushing in this article. I have encountered too many individuals who lost their enthusiasm along the way. The current system of hiring and employment in our world of K-12 does not encourage us to change, but I believe that changing jobs is helpful in minimizing burnout. I was fortunate enough to change jobs throughout my career, and I look back at the learning and experiences that I gained from it.

While at Watsonville High School, three teachers proudly boasted that they had 103 years of combined experience at that school. Some educators possess the resilience to endure the hardships of the job. Some school cultures provide important support for the entire staff to keep the positive juices flowing and to keep the enthusiasm level high! You can feel it when you walk onto a campus! What are the kids talking about? How does the facility look? How are you greeted in the office?

*When we are feeling enthusiastic, our brain experiences a flurry of activity involving various regions and neurotransmitters. Overall, when we are enthusiastic, our brain orchestrates a complex interplay of neurotransmitters and brain regions to create a state of heightened excitement, motivation, and positive emotion**

**OpenAI. (202). ChatGPT (Aug 14, 2024, version) [Large language model].*

Conclusion (for now!)

It is my belief that when leaders show sincere and demonstrable enthusiasm, the path to uniting people around a common vision is illuminated! What I have learned is that enthusiasm begets enthusiasm. We may encounter obstacles while striving to meet our goals. Many successful educators with whom I have worked are reflective of their actions and know tomorrow will bring a better outcome! They are aware of their own burnout and take steps to fix things, sometimes leaving the profession! Some folks can rely on incredible inner strength to keep a positive focus. Some simply know how to take rejuvenating vacations and return with fresh energy at the start of each new school year. Whatever you do, take care of yourself so you can take care of others! As you have heard from the flight attendants, they explain that you put on your oxygen mask before you help those around you!

My family provided the best support for de-stressing opportunities a busy principal could ever ask for! Watching them play sports, going on extensive travel vacations, reading to them when they were young…these activities and more helped me refresh and get up in the morning to begin anew! Sounds trite! However, of course, these activities and more helped my three children grow into superstars! I give my wife 51% of the credit for how wonderful they have turned out to be…but that is another story about raising a blended family!

Although I am not religious, I believe that we play a righteous role in our work in our public schools. Our doors are open to all. Educators with whom I have had the pleasure of working are the purveyors of hope. We can learn to predict a young person's success through the hope expressed by our young students. We, in education, provide hope for free! Hope and quality learning are achieved by the vast majority of our young folks. My Nobel Prize-winning brother and all of my family are products of public schools - Kindergarten through college graduation. (You didn't think I would conclude without dropping that one.) He and I have collaborated on our love and support of public education, and our concerns about limited resources and diminishing returns.

Our leadership repertoire needs to reflect the changes we experience in the world around us. We need to continue to grow in order to improve our surroundings and ourselves. In my career, the internet and the heightened use of social media have been two significant variables of change. However, the humanity of leadership remains unchanged. It's still about relationships, compassion, empathy, hopefulness, trust, vision, AND ENTHUSIASM!

Thank you for what you do today and tomorrow!

It's all about YOUR leadership!

Some Follow-Up ActivitiesDiscussion Regarding Your Leadership

1. Identify your mentors, even those who play a small role in helping you. What are their titles? How do they help you? What are areas that you would like help in from your mentors at this time?

2. How does your enthusiasm show up? What do people around you see and feel when you are enthused? Break into job-alike groups and describe what you see manifested in your colleagues' behavior when they are ENTHUSED!

3. Who are your key researchers at this time? What specifically do they offer you at this point in your career?

4. What systems are in place in your district or school site that reinforce positive behaviors?

5. What systems are in place in your district or school site that reinforce and enhance student learning?

6. How would you describe the CULTURE in your school? District? (Very general question!)

7. What is your routine in the morning to get you ready for work?

8. Do you have "triggers" that help you get upbeat and enthused? Share some examples!

9. If you wake up grumpy, what do you do to get yourself ready for work?

10. How do you plan for short-term projects? What about long-term projects?

11. How do you anticipate?

12. If you were to start a leadership meeting of some sort at your district or your school site, how would you break the ice to start the meeting? Do you have a good joke to tell?

13. How do you describe your leadership characteristics? Where do you want to grow? Now you can get specific!

14. What factors are you identifying that is keeping your leadership back?

15. How do you motivate your team?

16. What steps do you take to collaborate effectively with your peers?

17. How do you delegate tasks?

18. How do you encourage student development, both in personal and professional areas of their lives?

19. What leadership or professional development programs are participating in at this time?

References

[i] https://worldpopulationreview.com/state-rankings/per-pupil-spending-by-state

[ii] https://www.usnews.com/news/best-states/articles/2022-08-26/which-states-invest-the-most-in-their-students

[iii] Howard, T. C. (2010). *Why race and culture matter in schools: Closing the achievement gap in America's classrooms.* New York, NY: Teachers College Press.

[iv] https://www.youtube.com/watch?v=VKt9CslbVsg

[v] Colannino, Anthony (2021). *Leading with Head and Heart. Houghton Mifflin Harcourt*

[vi] Duncan-Andrade, Jeff, PhD. *Note to educators: Hope required when growing roses through concrete* Harvard. School of Education, Feb. 2010, YouTube Video: https://www.youtube.com/watch?v=8z1gwmkgFss

[vii] Shafer, Leah (July 2018). *What Makes a Good School Culture.* Harvard Graduate School of Education. *HTTPS://WWW.GSE.HARVARD.EDU/IDEAS/USABLE-KNOWLEDGE/18/07/WHAT-MAKES-GOOD-SCHOOL-CULTURE*

[viii] Epstein, Joyce (October 1997). *School, Family and Community Partnerships.* Barnes and Noble

[ix] Wingfield, R. J., Reese, R. F., & West-Olatunji, C. A. (2010). Counselors as leaders in schools. *Florida Journal of Educational Administration & Policy, 4*(1), 114-130.

www.ingramcontent.com/pod-product-compliance
Lightning Source LLC
Chambersburg PA
CBHW070916160726
48004CB00003B/1395